The DREAM
of Learning
Our
TRUE NAME

The Dream of Learning Our True Name

Kathy Galloway

WILD GOOSE PUBLICATIONS

Compilation copyright © Kathy Galloway, 2004
All poems copyright © Kathy Galloway, various years

First published 2004 by
Wild Goose Publications
Fourth Floor, Savoy House, 140 Sauchiehall Street, Glasgow G2 3DH, UK
web: www.ionabooks.com
Wild Goose Publications is the publishing division of the Iona Community.
Scottish Charity No. SCO03794. Limited Company Reg. No. SCO96243.

ISBN 1 901557 79 0

Cover graphic and map pages Photoshop work by Jane Riley

The publishers gratefully acknowledge the support of the Drummond Trust,
3 Pitt Terrace, Stirling FK8 2EY in producing this book.

A catalogue record for this book is available from the British Library.

Overseas distribution
Australia: Willow Connection Pty Ltd, Unit 4A, 3-9 Kenneth Road, Manly Vale, NSW
2093
New Zealand: Pleroma, Higginson Street, Otane 4170, Central Hawkes Bay
Canada: Bayard Distribution, 49 Front Street East, Toronto, Ontario M5E 1B3

Permission to reproduce any part of this work in Australia or New Zealand should be
sought from Willow Connection.

Printed by Bell & Bain, Thornliebank, Glasgow, UK.

CONTENTS

Remember me … 93

INTRODUCTION

In 1999, I visited a First Nation reservation in Ontario, Canada. There, I met three generations of women of one family, and heard something of their story. The grandmother and granddaughter both had names in their own First Nation language; the mother had an English name. As a child, she had been removed from her family and nation and sent to a Canadian mission school, where every effort had been made to erase from her memory all traces of her tribal identity, language and culture, and to assimilate her into the dominant Anglo-Canadian society around her. These efforts had been largely successful, and she spoke of feeling disconnected and alienated now from both cultures. She was also to a degree disconnected from both her mother and her teenage daughter; from the former because love was mixed with loss and ambivalence about the circumstances of her upbringing, from the latter because the young woman had rejected the assimilation forced on her mother and had identified strongly with her grandmother, learning, or relearning, the tribal language, customs and religious practices. This is not an uncommon story in Canada, but it was acutely painful to listen to.

The young girl told me how she came by her name. In accordance with custom, the name she was given as a baby was a temporary one. Her true name would be given to her in a dream, and she described the dream in which she had learned her name. This naming was profoundly important to her, both as the greatest signifier of her own personhood and as a marker of her identification with and as a member of her nation. The whole meeting echoed conversations I had had with the poet M NourbeSe Philip, an African Caribbean woman from Tobago now living in Canada, whose wonderful writing, especially in *She Tries Her Tongue; Her Silence Softly Breaks,* explores the struggle to find a language for naming reality when one's only language is that of the colonialist slave masters, the 'foreign anguish':

> *thisthisand   this*
>   *disfigurement this*
>   *dis*
>   *memberment*
>   *this*
>   *verbal crippling*
>   *this*
>   *absence of voice*
>   *that*
>   *wouldnotcould not[1]*

Perhaps the whole question of naming and being named is more immediate for women, who have to contemplate the possibility of changing their names in a way that men, as a rule, do not have to, and whose identity has undergone such shifts of meaning in the last century. But naming has always been significant, religious even. (Christians make a sacrament of naming, moving through the waters from a flawed identity to a new one, *'given in the rite, not constructed by negotiation and co-operation like other kinds of social identity'.2)* And it is not just a question of being known by others, of belonging, but of knowing oneself. Mary, stricken and bereft, looking for the lost Jesus in the garden, recognised him when he called her by her name. And in recognising Jesus, she knew herself again. She was Mary, the loved Mary, the recognised Mary.

The Scottish poet Kenneth White, whose work I love, and which awakens in me a sense of joyous optimism, is scathing about those whose writings consist of 'personal complaining and blunt generalities'. I fear that the poems in this book are not altogether free of either of these, for they are a kind of excavation of identity, and therefore deal with personal and political preoccupations (some might consider them obsessions!) such as gender and religious identity, maps, conflict, my relationship with Scotland's two largest cities, and a strange kind of theological geology.

In the ten years or so that these poems have been in the writing, the dream of learning my true name has changed in its character, and, without being at all convinced that I have learned it, I am content, as with grace, to receive it rather than to achieve it. I would like to think that, as Kenneth White writes:

'now the struggle at the centre is over
          the circumference
             beckons from everywhere'.3

But I fear this is wishful thinking.

I wish to thank several people who have nurtured the book to this stage without ever nagging: Alison Swinfen, for very helpful advice; Sandra Kramer and Jane Darroch-Riley at Wild Goose Publications for creative solutions; and especially Neil Paynter, for making me feel it has been a labour of love on his part, which is a great thing in an editor.

This book is dedicated, with much love, to four people who, in various ways, rescue me, often from myself.

Kathy Galloway

1 *She Tries Her Tongue; Her Silence Softly Breaks* by M NourbeSe Philip, Ragweed Press, Charlottetown, PEI, Canada, 1989.

2 Rowan Williams from *On Christian Theology*, p. 209, Blackwell Publishers, Oxford, 2000.

3 Kenneth White, from 'The walk along the shore' in *Open World: The Collected Poems 1960–2000*, Polygon, Edinburgh, 2003.

DEDICATION

for Molly, John, Graham, John

Real ...

REAL

I'm not a symbol
I'm not a statistic
I'm not the inches in somebody's column.

I'm not admirable, but
I'm not pitiable either.
I'm simply human.

If you turned me inside out,
you'd find fury, fear, regret and sorrow
struggling with the love and the longing,
hope and wonder,
and all my neediness.

Please take these things seriously.
Don't pietise or glamorise or trivialise or sermonise.
These are the marks of my life,
gift and loss,
wound and offence.
Please respect them.

I am at odds with all that requires me to be a symbol.
I insist on being real.

ANGEL-IN-WAITING

Stooping slightly to cross the threshold
through the low door,
you hesitate for a moment,
unsure of your welcome.
Silhouetted against the outside light,
a dark figure, sharp-angled,
not quite embodied,
yet you have an insouciant elegance
shrugged into the shoulders of the black coat
and in the long hair swept back from high cheekbones.
Your face is luminous,
your eyes kind and far-seeing
through this world and into others.

I love your companiable solitude,
your awkward grace,
your substantial transformations
in the planes of shape and shadow that flow from your fingers,
and, for all the tentativeness with which you inhabit this world,
the tough fibre of your love.

WINTER

It was a grey day.
Glasgow grey,
the rain getting in everywhere
and the sky as dreary as mince on a butcher's slab.

I was wishing to be walking among the painted houses of Stockholm
under a blue sky
because I could learn to love the winter there
where snow is crisp and leaves your shoes dry

or sitting in a tropical garden
watching lychees fall off the trees
under a scarlet sky,
heat steaming off the river, and my skin,
because I could forget the winter there.

North or south.
Anywhere but Glasgow really.

But then the kids came in and Duncan started an argument
about nothing, and about everything,

and we argued for hours, sitting round the table,
eating our dinner,
and after two hours Helen had gone away in a huff
because she wasn't getting enough attention
and David was looking for aspirin because his head was hurting
and I was collapsed on the couch from sheer exhaustion
and Duncan was standing there triumphantly, crowing,
about how he'd won the argument,
and it was so funny because all he'd done was worn us down
and we all ended up in tears from laughing

and I noticed that a bunch of tulips that I'd bought the day before
tightly closed
had opened in the warmth, and they were so beautiful,
and such a truthful colour of red-gold that I had never
in my whole life seen before, that for a minute
I couldn't breathe for it.

Then I was quite happy to be in Glasgow.

MY MOTHER'S DAUGHTER

Blue-glazed china and flowers in the room,
Red high-heels and expensive French perfume,
Green land, dancing, and a silver thread of song,
Food love and child love, sweet and spiced and strong.

In the matter of my life,
I am my mother's daughter.

HAIKU

your traces are everywhere
beauty is always with me
and love

HEREDITY

When I was a child,
my mother sang songs.
Old songs,
about good wives and fishwives and stockings of silk:
I know where I'm going, and I know who's going with me …
songs from the radio,
take my hand, I'm a stranger in Paradise …
and
que sera sera, whatever will be will be …
songs from the shows,
tonight, tonight, won't be just any night,
tonight there will be no morning star …
sacred songs,
I know that my Redeemer liveth …
My mother was always singing.

When I was a child,
my grandmother told stories,
about long-ago weddings
we drove round the loch in a pony and trap, and the driver
had
white satin ribbons on his whip
and brothers who went off to long-ago wars
that was your great-uncle Jack, he died in
the Boer War …
and never-met cousins in far-away places
there's Patsy in Melbourne and Harry in Canada …
and people she'd talked to in stations and tearooms
I met this awful nice young man while I was
waiting for the bus, he gave me his address
and asked me if I'd write to him …
My grandmother was always telling stories.

When I was a child,
my father was always going to meetings,
I'll be late tonight, Janet
getting people to do things,
believing that they could,
riding off on an old bike round the place.
Everybody knew him,
hi, Mr Orr …
implacable with MPs
that communist minister …
about the Bomb and South Africa.
When he had time, he followed the Hearts,
but my father was always going to meetings.

I see now that football
has been my main dissent from heredity!

EDINBURGH VIGNETTE

You're doing your Brownie Housewife badge.
Tidy these drawers, she said,
the public-spirited Morningside lady,
they're my daughter's.

I don't expect you've ever seen
so many nice things, she said,
to the ten-year-old from the housing scheme.

Oh yes, you said,
burning with indignation.
I have as many.

MY EDINBURGH

my Edinburgh is not Georgian elegance
re-presented in the confident, bullying classicism
of private schools,
public spirit
and the effortless identification of bourgeois taste
with revealed truth

nor is it the gaudy romanticism
of castles, medieval closes, old churches
dripping rotted flags
and the fake passions of underused imaginations
ejaculated every year
by the bucketful

my Edinburgh is the stench of the breweries
the view from the upstairs of a 27 bus
snowcemmed pensioners' houses
and a hard-on jabbing my thigh
against a wall behind the shopping centre

BIRTHDAY WISHES

(for Lorn)

Some kids get lullabies
They have their place
For keeping you quiet
With a dream on your face
And some kids get silver
For wishing them wealth
Or toasted in champagne

To drink to their health
And fairy godmothers
Showering blessings galore
And I wish you all these
But I'd add something more
A passion for living
That comes from your soul
And lets you get lost in
An ecstatic drum roll.

INCARNATION

Did you not feel the soft baby skin pressed to your cheek,
the small arms clinging round your neck like ivy on a post
the small weight asleep on your chest in the night,
and *know* that this was the meaning of the Incarnation?
This sweet, damp flesh, these small bones,
Christchild,
human,
the whole universe in her eye.

A few nights listening to the breathing of a sleeping child
could have answered a lot
of your endlessly tortured questions
about the doctrine of man.
You might have adapted your breathing
to the heartbeat of God
lying beside you,
and others might have killed
less babies.

A MAP OF BREAD

In Nazareth, Israel, warm, unleavened flat bread
eaten with hummus and olives
and local Palestinian dignitaries;
served with courteous formality,
the hospitality of the dispossessed,
and passionate subtexts.

In Phoenix, Mauritius, crusty baguettes
steaming from the oven of a Hindu baker
in a dusty Moslem town,
eaten with Chinese Christians,
a colonial legacy
to a multi-ethnic present.

In Sarajevo, Bosnia, pitta bread, kebab,
tiny cups of strong, sweet, cardamom-spiced coffee.
The crowded, cosmopolitan streets of this city
where Islam is at home,
a European faith,
buzz with conversation and culture heady in its richness.
But the still-shattered houses and charred hotels are silent witnesses
to a more brutal reality
and the potholed roads carry warnings
of landmines a few feet away.

In Moscow, Russia, solid, densely textured white bread
with crunchy cucumbers.
The June trees green in the city
and perestroika is in the air.
Women professors talk of fashion

of men who drink too much
of their children
of the rumour of possibilities.

In Naha City, Okinawa, not bread but rice,
pure white, unseasoned;
the Indians carry little pots of chilli to all the meals.
In the breakfast queue, the revolutionary leader in exile
speaks in measured tones of the slaughter of his people,
250,000 of them, invisible to western eyes.
Last year, fifteen years and many deaths later,
he finally went home.

In Harare, Zimbabwe, sticky sadza,
mealie porridge eaten with beautiful young women
who unaccountably die
between one meal and another.
Street children at the orphanage plant trees,
orange and lemon because 'there is no money for fruit'.
Harvest will not come in time for them.
They are planting for the future.

In Toronto, Canada, in a shop with eighty kinds of bread,
a man screams obscenities, threatens inexplicable violence
to the Korean shopkeeper.
She does not know him, nor any reason for his assault
but his hatred is palpable,
infects the other customers with fear.
Perhaps she did not have the bread
he was looking for.

'You shall eat, but not be satisfied,
and there shall be hunger in your inward parts.'*

On the map of bread
so many hungers.

And we, the satiated,
the powerful
of state and church alike,
having bread,
decide who shall eat
and who shall go hungry.

*Micah 6:14

Peace processes …

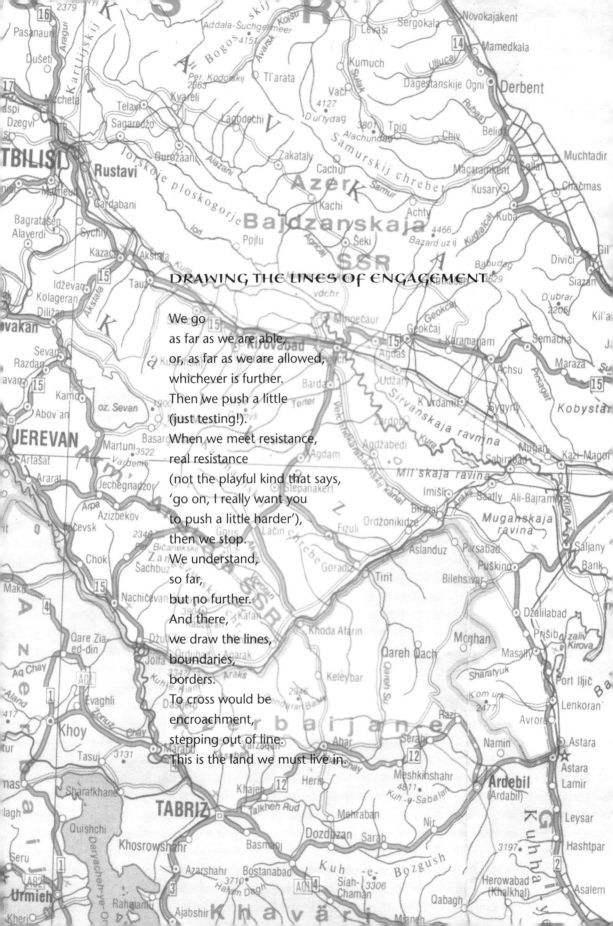

DRAWING THE LINES OF ENGAGEMENT

We go
as far as we are able,
or, as far as we are allowed,
whichever is further.
Then we push a little
(just testing!).
When we meet resistance,
real resistance
(not the playful kind that says,
'go on, I really want you
to push a little harder'),
then we stop.
We understand,
so far,
but no further.
And there,
we draw the lines,
boundaries,
borders.
To cross would be
encroachment,
stepping out of line.
This is the land we must live in.

BALANCING ACT

balance of power

I can live at peace
within these lines

I can live at peace
within these lines

imbalance of power

these lines are an iron
collar round my neck th
ey are choking the life
out of me till I can't sc

these lines may choke you
but they are necessary fo
r my security these lines
must stay as long as I fe

imbalance of power

I want more leeway do
n't be so inflexible th
ey're just little adve
ntures why can't you t
rust me more you're so

these lines are frighteni
ng me you keep breaching
them violating them I am
scared you will roll over
me entirely and I will di

balance of powerlessness

but I can hardly see t
he lines they are so f
aintly drawn I will no
t know when I am breac
hing them if you offer
me no clarity I don't
know where it's safe t
o go I'm lost and all
I do is wander in conf
using circles that det

why don't you observe the
lines you are not being f
air to me I never know wh
ere the next incursion is
coming from I am restrict
ed to a guarded immobilit
y seeing threats from all
directions holding on wit
h only instinct to a tiny
piece of ground I cannot

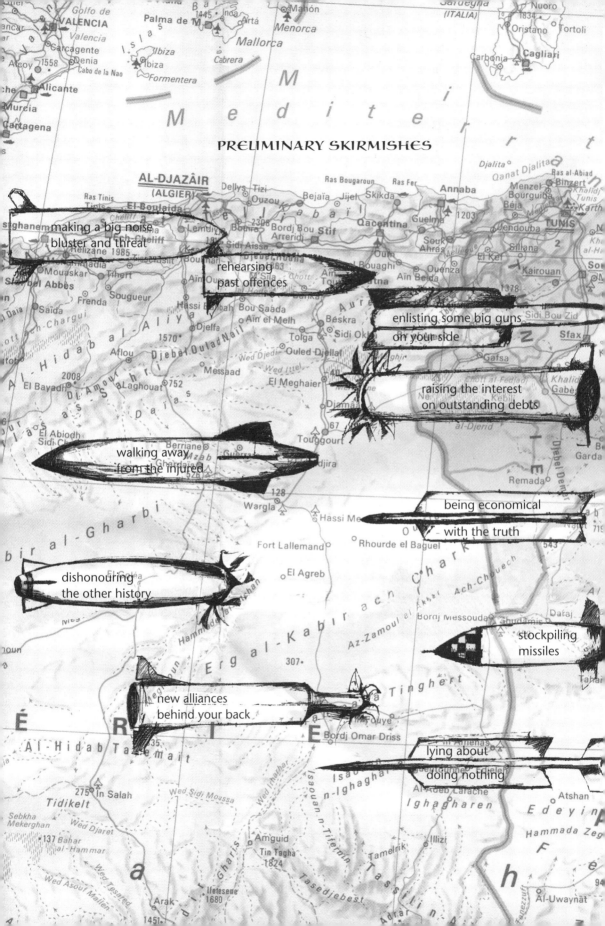

PRELIMINARY SKIRMISHES

making a big noise
bluster and threat

rehearsing
past offences

enlisting some big guns
on your side

raising the interest
on outstanding debts

walking away
from the injured

being economical
with the truth

dishonouring
the other history

stockpiling
missiles

new alliances
behind your back

lying about
doing nothing

OPEN WARFARE

the crunch of things breaking
the earth heaving up entrails
blood dripping into the ground
a child sobbing

the zen of war
(to be most lethally accurate
aim wide of the target)

the correspondents duck
in the lobby
the Red Cross waits

COUNTING THE DEAD

innocent (adj.) from in- 'not' + nocentem (nom. nocens),
prp. of nocere 'to harm'.

innocent 1. devoid of moral stain of blemish; blameless
innocent 2. not guilty of some specific sin, crime or fault
innocent 3. not tending to evil; morally harmless
innocent 4. ignorant of evil; simple, ingenuous, guileless
innocent 5. foolishly simple, ignorant
innocent 6. free from hurtful properties
innocent 7. a simple, harmless adult or child

the innocents

CEASEFIRE

Ceasefire.
Cessation of hostilities.

Neither side will plant bombs that go off
without warning,
traumatising everyone within range,
causing maximum damage,
leaving shards and splinters that
twist and throb in the flesh
for an unexpectedly long time
and require much gritting of teeth,
biting of bullets,
to be dug out from under the skin.

Nor will there be sniping,
scattershot,
stone-throwing
or roughing-up.

Outright intimidation will cease.
There will be a guarded neutrality,
fallback positions
will be fallen back to,
and the space between the lines
will be heavily policed.

The preconditions for negotiations
about negotiations
are now in place.

It isn't peace.
But at least nobody will get killed.

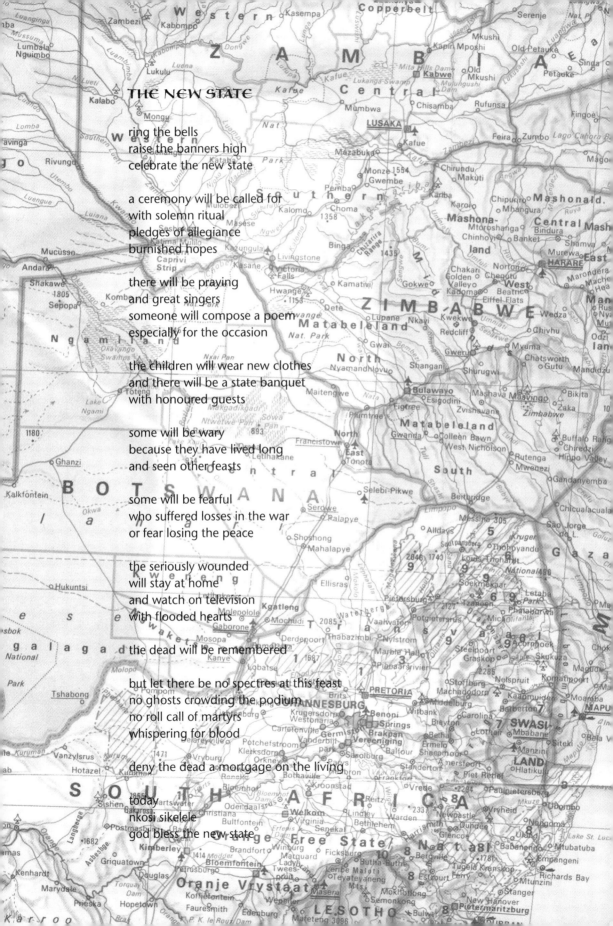

THE NEW STATE

ring the bells
raise the banners high
celebrate the new state

a ceremony will be called for
with solemn ritual
pledges of allegiance
burnished hopes

there will be praying
and great singers
someone will compose a poem
especially for the occasion

the children will wear new clothes
and there will be a state banquet
with honoured guests

some will be wary
because they have lived long
and seen other feasts

some will be fearful
who suffered losses in the war
or fear losing the peace

the seriously wounded
will stay at home
and watch on television
with flooded hearts

the dead will be remembered

but let there be no spectres at this feast
no ghosts crowding the podium
no roll call of martyrs
whispering for blood

deny the dead a mortgage on the living

today
nkosi sikelele
god bless the new state

DE-CONTAMINATION

In Cambodia
women pick their way through minefields.
They have been trained by aid workers
in the useful domestic skill
of defusing landmines.

Working in teams of twenty,
they can clear an acre
in two months.
Inch
by
inch.

Naturally, there are accidents.
A foot here,
a hand there,
or a life.

But they don't have any choice.
They need the land
to feed their children.

ALLIES

After the war
there is nothing
that does not require
to be renegotiated.
Nothing.

'How?' is important.

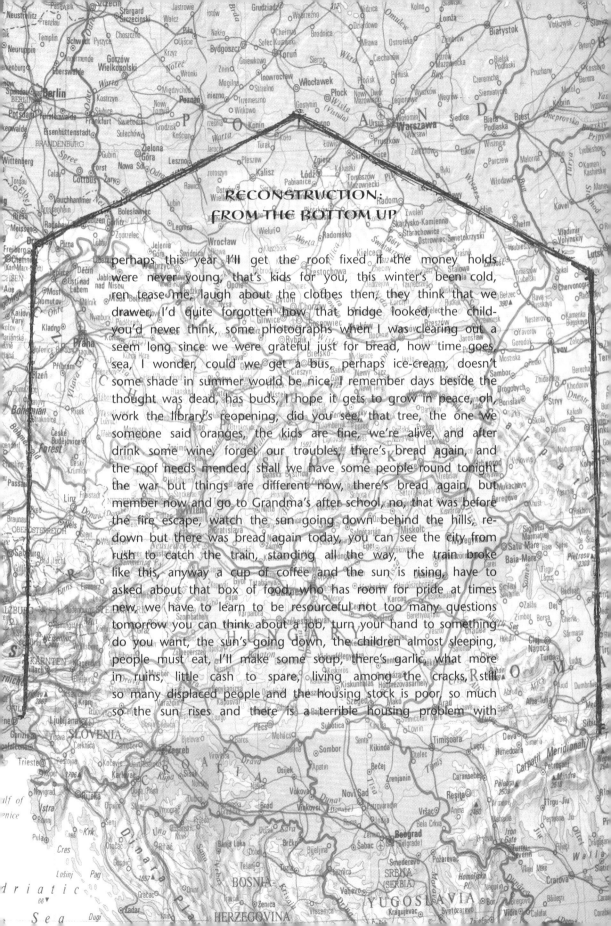

RECONSTRUCTION:
FROM THE BOTTOM UP

perhaps this year I'll get the roof fixed if the money holds
were never young, that's kids for you, this winter's been cold,
ren tease me, laugh about the clothes then, they think that we
drawer, I'd quite forgotten how that bridge looked the child-
you'd never think, some photographs when I was clearing out a
seem long since we were grateful just for bread, how time goes,
sea, I wonder, could we get a bus, perhaps ice-cream, doesn't
some shade in summer would be nice, I remember days beside the
thought was dead, has buds, I hope it gets to grow in peace, oh,
work the library's reopening, did you see, that tree, the one we
someone said oranges, the kids are fine, we're alive, and after
drink some wine, forget our troubles, there's bread again, and
the roof needs mended, shall we have some people round tonight
the war but things are different now, there's bread again, but
member now and go to Grandma's after school, no, that was before
the fire escape, watch the sun going down behind the hills, re-
down but there was bread again today, you can see the city from
rush to catch the train, standing all the way, the train broke
like this, anyway a cup of coffee and the sun is rising, have to
asked about that box of food, who has room for pride at times
new, we have to learn to be resourceful not too many questions
tomorrow you can think about a job, turn your hand to something
do you want, the sun's going down, the children almost sleeping,
people must eat, I'll make some soup, there's garlic, what more
in ruins, little cash to spare, living among the cracks, still
so many displaced people and the housing stock is poor, so much
so the sun rises and there is a terrible housing problem with

CROSS-BORDER PEACE TALKS

(dedicated to the Corrymeela Community)

There is a place
beyond the borders
where love grows,
and where peace is not the frozen silence
drifting across no man's land
from two heavily defended
entrenchments,
but the stumbling, stammering attempts of long-closed throats
to find words to bridge the distance;
neither is it a simple formula
that reduces everything to labels,
but an intricate and complex web of feeling and relationship
which spans a wider range than you'd ever thought possible.

That place is not to be found on the map
of government discussions
or political posturing.
It does not exist within the borders of
Catholic or Protestant,
Irish or British,
male or female,
old or young.
It lies beyond,
and is drawn with different points of reference.

To get to that place,
you have to go
(or be pushed out)
beyond the borders,
to where it is lonely, fearful, threatening,
unknown.
Only after you have wandered for a long time
in the dark,
do you begin to bump into others,
also branded,
exiled,
border-crossers,
and find you walk on common ground.

It is not an easy place to be,
this place beyond the borders.
It is where you learn that there is more pain in love than in hate,
more courage in forbearance than in vengeance,
more remembering needed in forgetting,
and always new borders to cross.

But it is a good place to be.

Let us be different ...

THE CRACK

There is a
crack.
Jagged and
long and
very deep.
The crack
is bleeding
having been torn
a howl
comes from its
heart
how to get back
together
with the proper fit
in right
relationship

the sides will not dovetail	neatly into place
too much of the edges	having crumbled away
nor can they	be forced together
without killing the fragile	flowers that cling to them
the crack	is permanent
one must, however, stand	on either side
as if it were not there	(although it is)
(knowing it is)	within the good
loving the other	in its absence
whichever side it is	embracing it
without that	crucial, agonising coupling
there is	only
the barren landscape of despair	the blackened territory of madness

trust the crack
it wants to be
a wild, luxuriant valley
with waterfalls
a river running through it
and on either side
fertile   fruitful
lands.

WALK ON

I am stubborn.
I will not give up.
Inching my way along the knife-edge,
crawling towards the vortex,
trusting the crack,
I head for the eye of the storm.
Each breath, I act.
I have staked my life on this.
The only release is no release.

THE LINE

Because I love you,
I will draw a line between us,
and over this line
I will not go.

Beyond the line,
in the space which is around you,
and which is yours,
lie your decisions,
your responsibilities,
your promises,
your power.
Yours, not mine.

Beyond this line,
if you struggle, I will not help you,
if you are sad, I will not comfort you,
if you are attacked, I will not rescue you,
if you are lonely, I will not be your company.

I will not weaken you,
shield you,
divide you from yourself.

Because I love you,
I will not cross the line to save you.

And if, encouraging from the other side
I see you look towards me once too often,
I will turn, and walk away.

Because I love you.

THE LINE TOO

But there is also this:
though I will not always agree with you,
I will always take you seriously.
If people speak ill of you in your absence,
I will say the good I know of you.
And though my weeping for your pain may be silent,
my delight in your accomplishments will never be.
Sometimes I will play around the line,
like a cat,
twisting in and out of unravelling wool.
And sometimes I will push hard up against it,
and if you are doing the same,
we will be very close;
as close as breathing.

And if, by chance, I should meet you in the street,
then a shiver of delight will race through me like the
hot silent shriek of ecstasy,
melt my casually cold-stored heart,
and leave me smiling at the great good fortune
that put us on the planet
at the same time,
and made our paths to cross
when we could, so easily,
have missed each other.

Because I love you.

FIGHTING TO STAND

The first time I saw you,
shock blasted through me
and I was afraid.

Being who I am,
that is,
attracted by danger,
drawn towards the edge,
rushing headlong towards the crack,
I desire to plunge headlong into the fear,
immerse myself,
swim about in it,
make its unfamiliar waters mine.

But, being who I am,
that is,
constrained by carefulness,
respectful of territorial rights,
regarding of the consequences
(to myself and others)
I scream to a halt at the edge,
and dabble my toes in the water,
test it cautiously,
draw back when I get out of my depth.

And, being who I am,
that is,
fiercely analytical,
self-witnessing,
conscious of my consciousness,
I observe myself, caught,
too careful for abandonment,
too passionate for calm detachment,
poised precariously on the edge,
struggling for balance.

Perhaps the shock
is not so much your otherness,
that sense of different worlds
whose language I have no command of,
whose outlines bear no recognisable landmarks
(though these might be enough,
so far it is to travel even to their borders).

Perhaps the shock is more a recognition
of someone else
balanced on the knife-edge
fighting to stand.

STANDING AND FALLING

I know,
in theory,
that there are times when it is
safe to surrender,
all right to let go,
delightful to give in,
but I have been on guard
for so long now,
I've lost my instinct
for telling the difference between threat and promise.
I have so much to lose.
It may not look like much to you,
but every square inch of my solid ground
has been hard-won.

I am tired
of being careful all the time.
But weariness is not to be equated
with good instincts.
So I am practising
little abandonments,
small surrenders,
learning to trust my instincts once again.
When the time comes,
I will be ready,
but not till then.

In the end, you just have to jump.
But I won't be pushed.

WHEN

When the long weariness
and the old hurts
finally start to unwind like a
knotted gut unclenching
on stepping on to solid ground
(which ground we are urgent to kiss)
after a perilous voyage
or like a voluptuous cat stretching and
moulding itself to the contours
of the rock upon which it will
best attract
and absorb the high sun of noon
having abandoned itself to the
absolute necessity of
stretching and
moulding and
abandoning
or like the sudden moment of
perfect spentness that follows
grief or fury or work or
courage or
love that has gone to its utter extremity
and breached that wall too
and is the field of the soul harvested
and ploughed
the now lies empty
open
waiting to be seeded

in these times

of unwinding

abandoning

spending

is felt the stirring

of a new

(or long forgotten) movement

coming up

through the ground

through the rock

through the field

through the tingling soles of the feet

through the liberated loosened muscles

through the fire in the belly

through the blood in the veins

through the drumming heartbeat

through the shoulders of I will

through the quickened and tantalised mind

through every nerve-end, sense and instinct

gathering momentum

till it floods and surges out

in a great green drowning wave

of gratefully uncontrollable

life

idea

imagination

design

desire

novelty   passion

poetry

care   creation

energy

spirit

form

harmony

shape

anger

colour

song

love

rhythm

and the silver Ariadne's thread showing us the
way back home is the same thread that invisible
led us by strange routes here and held us
connected with everything including the stars.

THERE WILL BE PEACE

In laughter I will find you,
So many joys I have shared with you,
They will become the measure of our time,
And there will be love between us
And there will be peace between us.

In tears I will find you,
So many times I will have cried for you,
I will offer you my song to ease your pain,
And there will be love between us
And there will be peace between us.

In anger I will find you,
So many times I have hated you,
But your tenderness will disarm me,
And there will be love between us
And there will be peace between us.

In losing you I will find you,
So many times I will be without you,
But things that you have given will not leave me,
And there will be love between us
And there will be peace between us.

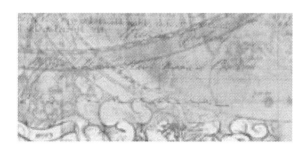

LET US BE DIFFERENT

Let us be different,
Let us not be the same,
You will be you, I will be me,
Each of us has our own name.

You do things your way,
In the light you have found,
You must be true to what you know,
And stand on your own ground.

Until we can learn
To honour each other,
To hear and know what makes us real
We can't love one another.

But when that time comes,
Though many the flowers,
From different roots, we shall be shown
That one earth is ours.

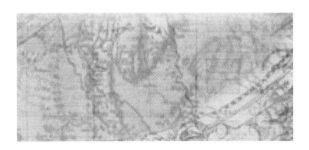

GOING OVER

You have burned your bridges.

You have passed through the gate marked 'no return'
and for you there is no going back.
No going back to the security of the known, familiar house,
to the well-worn dispensations and the threadbare coverings.

Now you are out there in uncharted territory
heavy with threat and shadows not yet entered.
The risks are high, and yet you strike out boldly,
guided only by unwavering conviction
and the longing for the true centre of the land.
This is what it means to do a new thing.

So, you travel lightly.
You are abandoned, given up in all things
to the task that lies ahead.
Therefore, you may be exactly who you are.
You have inhabited yourself,
you are at home,
and home is where you are,
even if it is the desert.
No one can dispossess you of your own in-dwelling.
This is what it means to be free.

We stand, one foot upon the bridge,
wondering if we too have the courage to go over
and strike the match behind us.

Rushes ...

(for Tony)

These poems were written a few years ago when I was involved in the making of a BBC television series called 'The Story So Far'. Each programme visited a place with some significance in the Celtic history of the western fringes of Europe and, in each, the story of the place was interwoven with the story of a present-day inhabitant of that place, and a story that Jesus told. In reflecting on these stories, I realised that I too, along with others who were part of the production, was being woven into this continuing story. Rushes are the first unedited prints of a scene or scenes shot for a film or television programme.

RUSHES

Whithorn: The sower and the seed

Rushes of red and gold sweep us through an empty landscape
dotted with white houses,
grey, slaty hillsides,
fat cows grazing incuriously,
down secret roads to the sea.
There, on a high cliff,
in a tomb,
in a walled garden,
among the ruins of another prosperity,
we talk of death and strange vanishings;
dig into the earth of our experience;
and the sky weeps on lost children,
smiling passions
and a dismal sea.

HERSTORY

Greyabbey: The final judgement

In a gracious house of the Ascendancy –
rolling parkland, stately trees, horses, gun dogs,
fine shabby furnishings –
tranquil on a vivid dappled day,
light washes us like linen,
clean and pale and soft with time.
We are gentle, and so
the crack of grief and death and bullets
and blood on a young woman's hands
from a boy father's wounds
is as intrusive as the planes that clog the sound waves.

What grace, to walk among the shattered fragments of a life,
to tell in minutes what cost years and weeks and days
and hours and minute by minute by minute piecing
back together of the years.
This woman, place, house, country,
inextricably tangled together by blood and greed,
complexity and complicity,
hatred and memory.
Also, the careful, slow, undemanding love of strangers.
They are the same story.

GIFT

Glendalough: The prodigal son

When I can't sing the deep valley of contentment,
I can sing stone on stone on stone on a rocky hillside.
When I can't sing the lake's reflective stillness
or the steady onward flow of the river,
I can sing the whirlpool of confluence
and the dappled bones of drowning leaves.
When I can sing neither the church of women,
huddled and overlooked,
nor the dominant isolation of the high tower,
guarded and watchful,
I can sing the lean grace of cave and cell,
and the world held in a single golden leaf falling
softly, soundlessly, unhurriedly,
gently breathed to the ground whereon
we walk.
And when my voice is silenced,
a distant accordionist playing vulgar tunes of
communal joy
will give melody to all that I
(although not he)
can see.

SCHOLARSHIP

Llanychtid: The parable of the talents

'If a thing's worth doing, it's worth doing well.'
So my mother told me,
and here, things are done well.
We are well-schooled
in the arts of living,
and the tongues of men and angels
get plenty of practice. This is good.
But,
'if a thing's worth doing, it's worth doing badly.'
This also is true, as Jesus observed.

I will not send my son here.

HEWN FROM ROCK

Pendeen: The workers in the vineyard

Hewn from rock.
Leaning, luminous graves;
church and parsonage, hard, eccentric Victorian elegance;
men, lives half-underground;
faith, to move mountains and bury babies.

In my mind's eye, I see the rock
under its gentle covering of green hedges,
fluttering curtains, heritage centres,
chocolate cake.
I like this place.
The rock remains.

LEPERS

Carnac: The Magdalen chapel: The great feast

At the great feast there will be oysters,
and moules à la crème,
and the driest white wine,
and I will converse animatedly with my neighbour
(who will be very handsome).

THE STORY SO FAR

The connection between the world
that pushed men to the Atlantic fringes
to make a heart out of a quiet cell
and this one where we arrive in cars,
wrestle through the night to make things work
and grumble over breakfast,
is not immediately apparent.
But it's there.
In part, it is the ground we stand on,
the same rock, tree, water.
But mostly, it's the story;
story seen, story heard, story lived.
The difference is mainly in the technology.
The connection is the story.
And this story is the harvest of that story.

Our true name ...

THE DREAM OF LEARNING OUR TRUE NAME

In the beginning
there was a dream …

We saw the four points
and from each one women were coming
and each one was bearing a burden

some were almost borne down by their weight
some stepped more lightly
one walked with children
but as they came
leaves and stones, flowers and berries,
bark and flame and grasses drifted around them
and woman who is a tree of peace
gathered them up
and shaped them into a sacred circle
and the women entered the circle
and we began our learning

woman with poems in her heart
taught us the art of receiving with grace

woman who remembers the future
taught us of silence, and fire in the snow

woman who gives power to women
taught us the necessity of practical responses
and to dare to wear flowers in our hair

woman who works from the heart
taught us that a clear mind is energising like cool water

... and there was not enough time
and there was all time ...

woman who points beyond
taught us to look with the eye of prayer

woman with the ocean in her soul
taught us the virtue of laughter in serving

woman who is a tree of peace
taught us to bend to receive earth's seasons

woman with fire in her heart
taught us to feel the heartbeat of life

... and there was not enough time
and there was all time ...

woman who brings forth healing
taught us attentiveness to the needs of others

woman whose heart is tender behind the shield
taught us that song is a wheel of fire

woman who makes everything beautiful
taught us how to bow to the universe
and to never, ever separate matter and spirit

woman who smiles through tears
taught us the cost of care
and the art of grieving

... and there was not enough time
and there was all time ...

woman who is sanctuary
taught us to ask the hard questions with kindness
and the importance of hugs

woman who gives voice to others
taught us how to hear the music beyond words

woman who walks with children
taught us the playful delight of creation
and how to let go

… and there was not enough time (for this is life)
and there was all time, for the circle goes beyond time
and in the time beyond time we dreamt a dream together
of the circle and the seasons
of the power of the waters
and the generations of humankind
of giving and receiving and suffering and learning
and the Great Spirit whispered our names in dreams
the name of all who love the mystery

and we saw with amazement
that everything we needed
was contained within the circle
all healing
all justice
all hope
all courage
all knowledge
a gift broken open before us
broken like bread
broken like loving hearts
broken like the life offered up
broken to be shared

and to give new life
if only we will receive it into ours
with open hands and a contrite heart

and we saw that the circle too must break
and there would be wide open spaces between us
but they will not be empty
for many, many people stand in them
and we are all part of the circle of life
and so we are not afraid
because we belong together in the circle
wherever we go,
and the Great Spirit who loves us
and has given us our true names
whispers them in the darkness
when we are alone
when we are weary
when we are despairing
and we are re-membered
in the heart of God.

CAMAS POEMS

Harry throws fire at midnight
on the green
and we are drawn from sleep
into an ancient dream of midsummer

the dark sea moves ceaselessly
its ebb and flow
is the ebb and flow of my blood
and is constant

far out in the bay under the moon
the *splish splish* of the paddle
is the sound of a sea creature
coming home

leaning against the stone walls of the house
in the time between
which is not day but is light
and is night but is not dark
we are bonded by our silence
silver threads of stillness weave us
into bright patterns of stars
shining on rocks and water
and shadows on the hill
and peace laps our souls

on the high cliff
our feet springing off heather and root

looking out over the sea
higher than the wheeling gulls
we are like gods
we might fly …

under the rafters
in the glow of candlelight
we break bread
and the word

to live is this

STONE HEART

… but I came to love my solitude, and
ranged across wide, empty hills, with heather
springing rough beneath my feet, barren land
of bracken-hidden tracks that led whither
they would, regardless of my choosing, till
the only way was down towards the sea.
I came there under a grey sky, and still
the leanness of the land delighted me,
seeing the stripped-back beauty of the bones,
the wind-whipped water and the stretch of sand,
yellow mosses, salt-damp, time-polished stones;
a stone-hard, soul-surrendered place to stand.

The shock is not that of invaded place,
but recognition of the cost of grace.

MANNA FROM HEAVEN

the circle of stones in the sand
will keep its shape only until
the tide washes over it
and tumbles the stones to a new beauty

desire too, white as the midsummer moon
or dark as pools on the shadowed side of the island,
has its ebb and flow

the eye that fills and the hand that trembles
are dry and still before the candles have guttered
and the ashes are cold in the grate

and intimacy is precious and fleeting as the scent of oil
on air and skin

we are going where it is not safe to dance with abandon and ecstasy
where we cannot laugh with trusting hearts
where prayer is not as uncomplicated as breathing in silence

but we will remember
that we ate manna from heaven
because we were hungry
and lived the truth of ourselves

of our need
and our sufficiency

The historic story of Christ, the outside story of Christ, suddenly emerges as the inside story of yourself – and it's this inner story, this inner parallel, that really makes the Bible inspired, so that to your condition it becomes the living word of God.

George MacLeod

Only forgiveness breaks the law of karma.

Raimundo Panikkar

Coming to Jerusalem …

SUNDAY: COMING TO JERUSALEM

We come with high hopes,
trailing expectations,
our own and others.
We come by many different means;
on foot, on horseback, some by sea, and some,
more lately, with removal vans.
We bear the weight of many histories;
strange lands, exotic memories, the scent of cumin
and the brightness of a Neapolitan sky.
We ask questions in Pentecostal tongues –
Gaelic, Irish, Cantonese,
in Yiddish, Polish, Urdu and Punjabi –
'who' and 'how' and 'what' and 'why'.
That's if we have the time and energy
to ask at all.
We come in exile from the jeer, the sneer, the midnight
   knock,
the dogs, the wire, the gas.
Or earlier, we run from fire and famine, so our children
   won't eat grass
and die like rabbits retching in a ditch.
We come because the old ways have departed
and sheep now reign where once the children played.
Old loyalties betrayed, old verities found wanting,
old certainties upturned, we come, cast out of Eden.

And tread our way among the crowds, in fear and
   fascination
of the city and its multitudes of possibilities.
Do we want to be here?
Perhaps.

But here we are regardless.
Seeking better times, polishing our hopes,
nursing our wounds, hiding all our doubts.

And somewhere in the corner of our mind,
suspicion flies to warn us that the gap between
our hopes and their fulfilment is somewhat large –
and slides away again.
All we have left behind us (or think we have);
the terror, rage, betrayal, death,
lie also in our future, here, among the shops and houses
and the heedless crowds.
There is no route that leads us back to Eden.
We must go on, and seek a more unvarnished,
    unacclaimed reality.
There are no shortcuts – this road's going all the way.

Catholic or Protestant,
Jew or Moslem,
Hindu or Buddhist,
agnostic or atheist,
it's all the same.
We're all coming to Jerusalem.
This is where there's nowhere left to run.
This is where we stand, and walk and fall, and (will we?)
    rise again.
There it is.
Pictured in the red and green and gold.
Welcome to Jerusalem.
City of …

MONDAY: UP AGAINST THE WALL

Up against the wall

Da da da da da!

That's the sound of machine-gun fire, staccato,
slamming you against the wall
and crumpling you down to the ground.

That's what I'd do to you,
you people who whinge about trivialities,
about your food, your comforts, your things, your
    precious privacy.

That's what I'd do to you,
you people who are wrapped in your smiling superiority,
you people who know all the answers and patronise
    the stumbling questioners.

That's what I'd do to you,
you people who are not serious about the suffering of
    the poor,
you who seek a soothing spiritual massage
or seek the safety of the sidelines to throw stones from.

You should thank God, you people,
that thoughts can't kill.
Otherwise you'd be spread-eagled, lifeless, on the carpet.

I would topple the idols, and you people who raise
  them up.
I would fling them down with fury.
And you must admit, there is a glorious finality about
  my anger,
even if a few innocent bystanders get caught by a ricochet.
My solution has enormous potential.
My anger has a huge scope.
It is almost unequalled as a cause of dispatch,
and has no need to be proportionate to the offence.

Of course, it does not require of me, in my imagination
  at least,
that I should cease to be merely human.
I would be god-like in my anger.

O God, the problem with my anger unleashed
is the same as that of my love tied up.
It puts me at the centre
and is the greatest idolatry.

Turn me over, Jesus,
Drive me out.
Cast me from your temple
Away from the house of prayer back to the streets and
  alleyways
Until my love grows at least equal to my anger
If not greater.

TUESDAY: AUTHOR-ITY

Some people want to eat their words.
Me, I'd rather regurgitate mine.
Throw them up. Flush them down the toilet.
Big words.
Long words.
Important words.
Poisonous words.
Difficult words.
'In' words.
In the words of the song, 'I'm so sick of words'.
'... just let me say this ...'
'... if I could get a word in edgeways ... '
'... you never listen to a word I say ... '
'... though I speak with the tongues of men and
      angels ...'
Passwords
Cover words
Swear words
Lying-in-your-teeth words

But without words
there are no stories.
Even the artist in the cave
had a word
to distinguish 'horse' from 'bull'
and so translate the images distinctly.

Perhaps the key is in the way you use them.

Is it kind?

Is it necessary?

Is it true?

To answer these requires the use of many more words

discerning words

listening words

evaluating words

'In the beginning was the Word. And the Word became
flesh ...'

I want to write my story in flesh.

Embody it.

Incarnate it.

WEDNESDAY: WHAT I KNOW NOW ...

It is the ache, the ache of weariness,
It is the longing, the longing for peace,
It is the separation, the separation from others,
and from you.

I know the ache of weariness – tired by the decisions that
                lie behind me
           – fearful of the choices that
              lie before me
           – wishing only for it all to be
              resolved, to reach an end
I offer you my decisions, and my fear, and my wish for
    easy endings.
I offer them in trust, for they are safe with you.
You understand my ache.

I know the longing for peace – to get away from the
                  endless demands of people
             – to lay down the burdens of
             responsibility
             – to escape the obligation of
             always having to be
             patient and explain.
I offer you the demands, the burdens, the obligations.
I offer them in trust, for they are safe with you.
You understand my longing.

I know the separation – feeling alone in a roomful of
people
– needing a friend in the struggle
– wanting more, yet not quite
knowing what

I offer you my aloneness, my struggle, my incompleteness
I offer them in trust, for they are safe with you.
You understand my separation.

Forgive me that my offering is so little.
I would have it more lavish, more extravagant.
I would have it be something you need or want.
But for tonight, it is all that I have to give.
Take it, then, my dear.
Incompleteness is given with all the love I have.

THURSDAY: DOING LOVE

There's only what you do.
Everything else is inside your head.

But, what you do is the expression
of who you are
and what you know.

You do your tone of voice.
You do the spaces round about you.
You do the silences between your words,
not just the words themselves.
You do the songs you sing.
You do the cup of tea you made your mum.
You do the way you spend your money
and the way you didn't spend it.
You do the love you make
and all the love you didn't make.
You do the atmosphere you change within a room.
You do the rocking of the baby in your arms.

It's what you do that carries me to you and you to me.

But, what you do is the expression
of who you are
and what you know.

If who you are feels wrong,
or not worth much,
then what you do will mirror that.
And you receive what others do
in that same way.

And if you think that what you know
is useless, not enough, of no importance,
then you'll do less than what you could,
or do it to convince yourself that no one else
has noticed what it is that you don't know.

The thing is,
you're all right.
You'll do just fine.

And what you know, till you know more,
is quite enough
for doing love.

FRIDAY: STATIONS OF THE CROSS

Jesus is sentenced to death

The moment you stood out,
the moment you refused any longer to conform,
to fade into the background;
the moment you stopped being nice
and got angry,
confronting us with what we knew about ourselves
but preferred to attribute to others;
the moment we realised that you meant not mastery
but freedom;
in that moment
you signed your own death sentence.

Jesus carries the cross

Your arms are strong.
They have cradled children.
They have broken bread and served it to your friends.
They have prepared a meal for countless empty bellies.
They have stretched to touch and raise and heal.

Your back is strong.
It has carried many cares.
It has bent to stroke a thousand fevered brows
and stooped to wash the dirt from dusty feet.
It has borne the weight of too much expectation.

Strong arms, strong back.
Strong enough for a cross?

Jesus falls for the first time

It's not that you didn't try.
It's not that you wouldn't have carried it
all the way if you could have.
It's just that you had to operate
within the limitations of your strength.
God knows you pushed them back again
and again.
More than you'd thought possible,
more than anyone could have expected.
You tried all right.
But in the end,
it all became too much for you.
It bore you down, and you stumbled, fell.
It's not that you didn't try.

Jesus meets his mother

Oh mother, oh mother.
Here is your hope, your joy, your pride,
staggering up a leprous road to meet you.
Here is your flesh, your blood, your opened womb,
here is your milk, your tears, your sleepless nights.
Here is the ache that rises from between your legs
and splits you upward like a gutting knife.
Here is your skin, the pulse you felt beneath your hand,
here are your eyes, your colour, and the unmistakeable smell.
Here are your dreams of feasting at a wedding.
Here is your youthful passion, and your dancing days.
Here is your finest fleshly imprint and your better self.
Here is your child,
staggering up a leprous road to meet you.

Simon of Cyrene carries the cross

You met each other as strangers.
That is to say, you both were strange.
One of you estranged by deed beyond acceptance,
the other picked unerring from the concealing crowd.
But both of you were used to bearing burdens,
had grown accustomed to the lash upon your back.
Was it strange, to know the greatest tenderness that there
    could be
would be to lean upon this strange man's strength?
How often did you ache to lean upon a strong man's
    strength
and find that all your men relied on you?
Strange that, at the end, such tenderness should come
in this strange way, from one a stranger to you.

Veronica wipes the face of Jesus

We know the agony of feeling useless.
We know the scream inside
of absolute and utter powerlessness.
It spawns within us, clawing, gnawing,
and it is fed by what we're forced to watch.
Our eyes grow fat on children's torture;
they swell on every bitter, pointless death.
They bulge with each unnecessary hunger
and vomit out the gross and stupid waste.
But screams are lost, and self-indulgent.

They do not help the helpless or assuage the bile.
And so we act, even while knowing that our act
is gesture, token, out of all proportion to the pain.
We take the towel; it is the only thing we have.
But still, a gesture, it is something, is it not?
It speaks of more we would do if we could.
It is more than nothing.
Isn't it?

Jesus falls for the second time

Embarrassment, because we know we should help.
Guilt, because we know we could help.
Self-delusion, because we know we would help
if only …

Lust, because we secretly enjoy the pleasure.
Anger, because our shame dispels the pleasure.
Nausea, because relief's a sickly pleasure
and yet …

Pity, because we are not dead to goodness.
Memory, because we once caught sight of goodness.
Desolation, because this wretchedness suggests the doom
    of goodness
in us …

What tangled feelings shimmer on the surface of this
    crowd
as, once again, we stand and watch you fall.

Women of Jerusalem weep for Jesus

They are disgusting, your tears.
They are so facile, maudlin, always on display.
You pour them out like water from a jug,
you squander them with little thought for what was paid
to set them flowing.
Save your tears, you daughters of Jerusalem,
and save your easy cheers as well.
Cheers, tears, it's all the same to you.
Emotions lightly conjured up to fit the given mood.
It is enough! Enough of borrowing the deeds of others
to satisfy your own vicarious needs.

Your acts are needed now, there has been too much of
    women weeping.
Dry your tears, resolve instead by your decision
that there will be in future fewer times
for grief like this.
Or, if you will not put your strength and courage
at the service of resistance to the powers,
then weep for your own children, for your daughters'
    daughters.
For, in truth, you will yet live to see them
crushed beneath the weight of mountains, hidden by
    the hills.

Jesus falls for the third time

How can you keep falling?
Why do you not rise?
You don't have to do this
you can lift your eyes.

Look beyond the mountain,
see the other side.
Throw the damned thing over,
why have you no pride?

Why must you keep falling?
Out there, there is space.
You don't have to be here,
you can find your place.
You can still be someone,
leave all this behind.
If you think they'll thank you
you must have lost your mind.

You could go on falling
from now till kingdom come.
Nobody will bother much,
they'll just think you're dumb.
But they'll be quite happy
to add more to your load.
How much more can you carry?
Do you think you're God?

Please don't go on falling!
It isn't right, you know.
They're getting off too lightly
if you let them use you so.
I don't know what you're doing
or why you're here at all.
I only know that this time
I can't bear to watch you fall.

Jesus is stripped of his robe

The silence is hot.
They're all attentive now.
The sweat is streaming.
The sweat is steaming.
The flush is rising.
The flesh is rising.
The eyes are shifting.
The eyes are drifting.
The heat is sullen.
The threat is sullen.

Gripped, ripped, stripped.
Now you are ready for action.

Jesus is nailed to the cross

Got you!
Now we're going to put you firmly in your place.

Did you really think that we would let you get away
with trying to challenge what has worked so well
and to the advantage of so many?

A little tinkering here and there – we can allow that.
We are very happy if you want to play with children
or entertain the women (though we would prefer it
if you don't reclaim too many prostitutes).
And healing, well, we all enjoy a happy ending.
Even feeding the poor saves us the bother.

But let me emphasise, there could be no allowance
for the real enormity of what you've done.
You cannot criticise the church.
You cannot undermine the state.
You cannot challenge the establishment
and expect benign approval.

Above all.
Let me hammer home the point …
You must not threaten or subvert the patriarchy.
Nor side-step altogether the balance of the powers.
How dare you be so impertinently alive?
That is to threaten God,
and we do not like that. Not at all.

So here you go.
Up against the wall.
Bang! Bang! Bang!

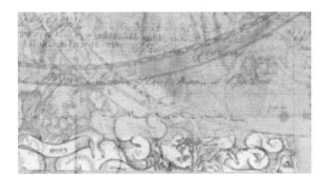

Jesus dies on the cross

Fingered

Taken

Stripped

Spread-eagled

Exposed

Humiliated

Whipped

Mounted

Violated

Broken

Jeered

Handclapped

Spat on

Cursed

Abandoned

Dead

Jesus is taken from the cross (pietà)

She will hold out her arms to you

She will take you upon her knee

She will turn your face to her breast

She will rock you and sing gently to you

She will smooth the hair from your brow

She will cover you against the chill air

She will kiss you goodnight

Children do not die to their mothers
Though the mothers should see them grow old
Though the knife should betray them
Though the flesh should decay
Though the memory grow old
Though the images fade
Though the pain engulf them.
Children do not die to their mothers.

Ask any mother.

Jesus is laid in the tomb

Will it come to this at last?
Will dreams grow cold? Will freedoms die
and come to lie in stone?
Will people pause in times to come
and wonder why you tried
to do this new thing, newly;
then shrug, and turn back
to the same old ways –
the same old, sterile ways?
Must flesh and spirit constantly
do battle for a worthless piece of ground,
contest false claims,
arrest each other,
do each other down to death?

Or will the day come ever
when they give up the struggle
and melt, instead, into each other,
and move, and glow, and love each other,
and slip the chastening chain that binds them,
dissolve the clay that blinds them?
And flow out of the door of no alternatives
and enter into time and space?

Such power, on such a day, would shatter opposites,
would split the rock, allowing you
to enter and reclaim your darling flesh.
The dead would rise!

But in the absence of surrender, and alternatives,
here is the stone.
Shut the door.
Go away.

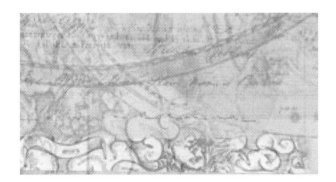

SATURDAY: SEND US AN ANGEL

… send us an angel that will start us seeking a new way of life …

George MacLeod

Birth and death come accompanied by angels.
And sometimes, maybe always,
the moment of encounter is the same.

Annunciation – 'you will be changed,
you will give birth to something new.'
And the guardians of the tomb –
'He is not here. Why do you seek the living among the dead?'

Lot or Lot's wife-like,
poised between no-longer and not-yet,
this I can understand.
This I can, albeit painfully,
give my assent to.

But why did no one warn me
how terrifying angels are?

They are not nice and reassuring,
all dressed in white.
They come with flashing eyes,
and carry flaming swords to pierce your heart.
They come with ruthlessness.

Still, they teach you one thing,
these messengers of God.

I have learned the proper fear of the Lord.

And with this fear, I wait for death, and birth.

SUNDAY: RESURRECTION

I do not know
what resurrection is
(though I'm almost sure
it has something to do
with hallowing the common ground).
Of course, that's not all of it.

I expect one day I'll get up
and find that it sneaked up on me
while I wasn't looking,
and maybe even that it's been there all along.
That's as may be.
There's no point in trying to see things
before you're ready.
You have to walk before you can run.

In the meantime,
I believe in it.
And that feels like an initial step.
For now,
it will do.
It is enough.

Remember me …

CHRIST OF SCOTLAND

He walks among the yellow and the grey.
Grey of stone and slate and steely rivers
running through grey towns where steel ran yesterday,
and grey mists lifting where the coming day
delivers grey-edged intimations of
a grey mortality,
and a shadier morality.
Here, poverty and pain are dirty-fingered currency
in the market-place of souls,
and stunted possibility hobbles on the bleeding stumps
of legs hacked off from under it.
Here, in the grey forgotten wasteland
that is not fate or accident or fecklessness
but just the grey, inevitable result
of choices made,
and burdens shifted,
and costs externalised out of the magic circle
of prosperity,
here, he walks.

But in his heart he carries yellow.
Yellow for the daffodils that surge across the banks
    of railway lines.
Yellow for the crocuses that parade in Charlotte Square.
Yellow for the primroses that gleam in crevices of island
    rock.
Yellow for the irises that wave from glittering ditches.
Yellow for the broom that flashes fire across a thousand
    summer hills.
Yellow for the barren land cloaked in winter snow,
awaiting yellow springtime's sun

to kiss it into bloom.
He carries yellow in his heart.
Held high like the lion raised upon the terraces.
Yellow for courage.
Yellow for beauty.
Yellow for resistance.
Yellow for love.
Yellow to obliterate the grey.
He walks, yellow, in the grey.

REMEMBER ME

Do you remember me?
Though I am nameless to you
and have no statue or square in my honour,
you will look down and I will be there,
under your feet,
close to the earth where I lived and died.
I could not rise where you might look up to me on a plinth or plate;
too many burdens pinned me down.
Narrow sunless streets and overcrowded closes hemmed me in;
I breathed damp and foetid air from running walls
and cholera, typhoid, tuberculosis, asthma laid me low.
Polio, rickets and poor food shortened my stature and my days,
and heroin and AIDS cut me down.

Remember me, do you?
I turned the wheels that made the engine-room roar.
I dug your roads and built your ships,
I carted your coal and drove your trains,
I forged your iron and unloaded your docks,

I stoked your boilers and fed your production lines,

I cleaned your offices and swept your streets,

I sewed your clothes and emptied your bins,

I made your weapons and fought your wars,

I fried your food and guarded your factories,

until you had no more use for me

and I became an economic liability.

I came from many places to do it:

from the highland glens and island shores,

from the slave-mines of Ayrshire and the valleys of Lanark,

from Ireland, Poland, Russia, Italy,

from India, Pakistan, Uganda, China,

from Chile, Vietnam, Iraq and Kosovo;

well that you remember me on the ground beneath your feet.

The city was built on my labour.

You remember me?

Remember the miracles I worked, on low pay, or no pay,

on strike pay or benefit.

Remember the washing I did,

walls, stairs, clothes, weans;

remember the lullabies I sang them when they couldn't sleep,

and the nights I sat up with a sick neighbour.

Remember the wakes when they died.

Remember the allotments I dug

and the jerseys I knitted

and the houses I painted;

remember the matches, the beautiful game.

Remember the singing, remember the dances;

remember the patter, and the drinking, and the laughter,

remember the courting and the weddings and the babies.

Remember the young ones who made it to college,

and the others who didn't, remember them too.

Remember the unions and the co-ops and the tenants' groups,
remember the marches to the Green and the Square.
Remember the suffragettes and the rent strikes, and the poll tax –
remember we tried and we fought and we cared.
Remember that I kept on getting up every morning,
remember my prayers and remember my tears.
Remember that I lived and my life had a value,
remember that I loved and hungered for more:
for the chance to reach out and look up and see further,
for a life free of want and exhaustion and fear;
for the right to be treated with justice and dignity,
for the right to be human,
for the right to a name.
It's not much to ask, but it's harder to come by,
and it's hardest of all to be seen when you're poor.
So when you walk by, just stop for a moment
and see me, and wonder, and maybe ask 'why?'
And *you* remember me.

(Written for the laying of a stone in George Square, Glasgow,
to commemorate all those who have been victims of poverty.)

REJOICING IN HEAVEN

She sings like a raucous angel.
The Blessed Patsy Cline of Pollokshields;
and heaven applauds.
Earth, on the other hand,
whose taste is in its arse,
has not been so appreciative,
and has rewarded her with
abusive men,
crummy houses,
rotten jobs
and a tendency to badmouth her
when she drinks too much.
However, I have it on good authority
that when Celia sings
saints start swaying their hips
and archangels go all dreamy.
They like a bit of attitude in heaven.

THE BOTANIC GARDENS IN WINTER

In the Botanic Gardens
a robin parades its rusty chest across my path
a swan drifts slowly sideways on the river
the sun makes a minaret-shaped pillar of light on the water
bare branches show their buds suggestively.
In the Kibble Palace
I wait to be soothed.
I think I might crawl in among the tree ferns
and lie down and die.

IN THAT PLACE

I used to live in a place where everyone
had been decanted.
(Funny word.
Did it mean we were like wine?)
Slum clearance, new hopes, high houses.
We used to hang about the chip-shop,
go into the woods and fool around,
wander the streets.
I liked it.
In that place I walked by flaming torches
and there was crisp snow under foot
and people hung out of their windows
to hear us singing.

I used to live in a place
where the toilet was on the stair,
the putrid smell of the horsehair factory choked the air
and, some Saturdays, junior Orange Walkers wakened me from sleep
with the sound of hatred made indescribable by its innocence
bereft of memory.
In that place,
I saw three boys
beat the Asian owner of the corner shop
with an iron bar
to the pavement.

I used to live in a house above a pub
and sometimes in the morning
there was blood on the tiles and the floor
from the stabbing of the night before.
Food was cheap, and men were

always getting laid off, and
violence lay close to the skin, always
ready to erupt like a red stain at the
slightest scratch.
In that place,
I heard a girl scream, and
saw a man rush from a close-mouth doing
up his trousers, and the girl stagger
out into the darkened, shuttered street.

I used to live in a place where dogs
hunted in packs and you had to watch
all the time where you put your feet.
And the houses were running with damp and the
children got asthma and bronchitis and
watched burning cars for entertainment.
In that place, loyalty was fierce and generous,
people had good parties and there was a
perverse pride that came from being
damned by poverty and prejudice.

I used to live in a place where the sea
was the undercurrent of everything.
The sea is more beautiful than anything in the world.
And grey stone dykes were the perfect expression
of a harmony of nature and culture.

And it would have been no surprise
to walk into another time,
because eternity was always promising
to break through time,
and sometimes did.
In that place,
I learned the intrinsic value of stones.

In the place where I live now,
Sumeira comes to play with painted hands,
Matthew bears five royal names of Africa
and Asoka folds fragile paper cranes.
I look out of a basement window
on trees, and many legs,
and make my way along the road,
waving to the fish-man and the pizza-man
and the girls who sell me olives.
In this place,
I love the flow of life
just waiting for the lights to change.

In all the places I lived,
there were people I loved.

I hate everything that damages people.

MEETING (1)

I met an old friend yesterday
on a traffic island in a busy road.
We hugged, smiled, exchanged news of children,
talked about our work.
Gladly I let a train go by, for I love this friend
and see him rarely.
For years we shared a house, a life,
were close; his wife and I were pregnant together.
He saw my antenatal scan, felt my bump,
four of us crowded into a small cubicle
with a slightly scandalised nurse.
Next week, on my birthday,
he celebrates his silver wedding.
We cannot believe it –
'where did the time go?'
The babies are twenty-one.
We kiss, and part.

MEETING (II)

'What do you think? What do you think?'
She is agitated, obsessive,
a bent little woman in a floaty skirt.
'Children should be taught about hell in Sunday School.
Otherwise how will they know that Jesus can save them when they die.'
Useless for me to point out that hardly any children
are in Sunday School these days,
or that frightening six-year-olds is possibly not the best way
to communicate a god of love,
or that fear of hellfire and damnation has darkened the psyches
and blighted the lives of too many Scots in the past.
I wonder if it has blighted hers.
She does not hear me.
'I'm glad I got taught about hell …'
And she wanders off muttering.
Why was this the question she most needed to ask me,
someone she hardly knows?

DREAMING OF EDEN (1)

I watch them sometimes,
couples in their fifties.
They seem vital, purposeful,
still sexual,
not yet having reached the time of
metamorphosis
to ungendered old age
or long widowhood.

Staying on the straight road,
they have negotiated a way through
the irritable dislike of early familiarity,
the exhaustion of young parenthood,
the absence of feeling that frightened one day.
He didn't go off with another woman
to try it all again,
she resigned herself
to weaving her work round his.
They are a triumph of adaptability.

Now is the time of bringing in the sheaves.
Children grown and gone,
more money, time
for travel,
good dinners,
old friends,
long-cherished plans,
pride in family
and the companionability of a lifetime.

It's not perfect.
So many losses.
But maybe
it's as good as it gets.

DREAMING OF EDEN (II)

no gays
(Adam and Adam!)

no one past childbearing age
or under the age of consent

nobody fat
(not naked!)

no one with parents
(conflict of loyalties)
and no siblings
competing for attention

no one with diseases

no one who is not a virgin

and definitely
no one curious

no wonder there were only two of them

DREAMING OF EDEN (III)

Dreaming of Eden
I conjecture you
knowing everything

Tumbling towards a hard outcrop
we land together like homecoming
and are withstood

Dreaming my mouth on your face
yours on the veins of my wrist
all our exiles return

Dreaming innocence
knowing everything
we are cursed
we cannot fall

TONE POEM

This one's a hearth.
Comfortable, well-banked,
with an occasional spark and crackle,
because fire is never entirely safe.
I warm myself at it,
and it melts the touch of frosting I carry in
from the cold outside.

This one is a blaze of berries on a green tree,
sappy and crisp with the tang of pearl-grey
early autumn mornings
through which scarlet glows to lift my spirit.

This one's an endearing hedgehog,
bristles defiantly out.
I am trying to stroke it gently
so it will draw them back
and let the tender flesh below appear,
delicately removing the odd spine that
sticks into my flesh from time to time.

This one is a shell,
small, curled, not gaudy on the outside.
You might overlook it on a beach.
But it repays more careful attention,
disclosing in its heart
swirls of coral
and the sound of the sea.

This one's a long, cool drink
(perhaps a snap of lime in it)
that I am sipping very slowly through a straw.
The more I sip,
the more I like it.

This one's a minefield
I am negotiating with extreme caution
(always half-expecting the next explosion
in my head).
With each piece of firm ground gained
I proceed with greater confidence.
This field has beautiful grass.

This one's a child let out to play,
shouting and jumping with glee,
and (too long cooped up)
slightly overdoing it,
as children will.
I want her to have a lot of fun.

This one's an apprentice sun.
Sometimes it gets clouded over,
sometimes it sinks very low,
sometimes it forgets to come out at all
(it's still getting used to being a sun).
But sometimes, it struggles through the clouds,
lifts itself right up there in the sky
and shines like crazy,
warming me through to the marrow in my bones.

This one is little crab apples,

sharp and sweet in the same bite.

The taste of honey lingers on my tongue

but there is an ache of bitterness in my throat.

Wild fruit,

and the tremor of an angel

is this one.

This one's an exhilarating walk

in stormy weather,

ranging over springing moorland

scented with bog myrtle

all the way to the sea

and a wander along a beach

of white sand, driftwood and rock pools.

It is a source of some delight to me

that the more I go on,

the more differentiated,

complex

and yet flexible

becomes the feeling tone of love;

deeply responsive,

highly impulsive,

widely expressive;

subtle

and beautifully simple.

THE LIFE OF STUFF

I like your hands.
When you talk,
having become absorbed, and so
not self-conscious,
they have an instinctive gesture –
wide-open, palms down,
drawn towards the life of stuff –
like a priest at the epiclesis.
It's a hands-on gesture,
not just touching but transforming.

I see you playing your guitar
and your hands make shapes and movements,
interpret what you hear and feel, and
what you want to hear and feel.
Or with a camera, translating what you see
and what is waiting to be seen anew,
the eye still needs the hand;
reluctant subjects, in their hearts,
know the fear of revelation.

I imagine you at work,
working with paint or clay,
and I feel them, resistant yet malleable,
passive, yet always on the edge of transformation.
Or with a hammer and nails,
or with your child,
a 'hands-on' father.
Never think this is not worth more than anything.
Human stuff is the most precious,
the strongest work.

I would like to be a fly upon the wall
and watch you work, unseen.

When you talk about your work,
you are a different person.
Relaxed, not worried, accepting.
You should trust your work.
Theories have their place but love is concrete,
lets you be yourself,
and you love through your hands.
Trust your hands.
They have a true instinct
for this alchemy,
this transforming process in the life of stuff,
this sacrament,
this whole, this holy thing.

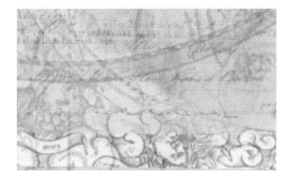

ELEMENTAL

I am earth.
Dark and sticky and fecund.
Nameless things wriggle and turn in me,
I am their habitat,
and it is only a habit of thinking
that calls them ugly, dirty, slimy.
They are what they are, have their genesis,
and in my inmost depth
they too are being changed,
uncurling their potential.
I think this is love.
To contain the transforming power of life.

I am fire.
Hot and sharp and bright.
Some days I trickle through the curtains early
to keep me going till noon
though I only notice me for half an instant.
And sometimes I am fierce and focused
showing me something previously unseen.
But on the best days
I am the heat that warms my blood
and stretches me out, lazy and loose
like a cat reclining on a stone.
It is love, the fire of your life.

I am water.

Wet and runny and cool.

Almost every part of me.

I sink in myself each moment,

I am inside and outside,

ingesting, expelling,

I am wine, I am tears,

I am the sea that I surge in

and the sea that surges in me

and the gleam on the mud and the love

of the puddles of my daily life

and the sludge is the water of life.

I am air.

Empty and teeming and charged.

Atmospheric,

heavy and heady and thick

or restless and rushing about

upsetting the balances, out of alignment.

Smoke hangs upon me and dust chokes my throat,

but suddenly, out of thin air

I am lucid, transparent and still, I am still

loved, and love is the

air that I breathe

and I am the air that breathes me.

HUMAN (TRANSITION)

can't go forward

can't go back

can't go home

can't go out

can't cross over

can't stay here

this is time

this is no time

this is place

this is no place

this is choice

this is no choice

help me

don't help me

hold me

don't hold me

tell me

don't tell me

inter/section

inter/face

inter/ruption

no good

stuck.

have to
transpose
into a
different key
explode
on to a
different plane
expand
into a
different dimension.

Yes!
Now we're in business.

fERA NATURAE

In my middle years, I am turning feral.

I pace out the boundaries of my territory,
putting my mark on it,
attentive to its changes.

I live underground,
take feeding seriously,
sleep on the floor
and am accessible only when I choose.

I love my young fiercely,
we nuzzle and scratch
and they cling upon my back.
Each day I undertake their providence
and their weaning
without regret.

I am body – brain and guts and spirit,
bone and blood –
flexing strong muscles,
powerful,
bearing happily my scarification and ageing.
One day soon, I will simply be
with no ghost to note my being.

At night, I sniff the wind:
roasting meat,
sweet fermented yeasty smells,
smoke and green smells,
and the male of the species.
Do not be deceived by my placidness;

I am self-contained within a stalking circle,
and if you have good hearing,
you will hear me growl under my breath.
I am
lying in wait
predatory.

I am the property of no one,
obedient only to my creation.
I am unpossessed,
fera naturae.

RESOLUTIONS

to be absorbed
– eating an apple
– watching a worm cross my path
– talking to a friend on the phone
not to be always walking along behind myself

to be supported
– letting someone carry my bag without a second thought
– letting someone love me without calculation
– letting life carry me to its next destination without a timetable
not to be always determinedly making life bearable

to be ecstatic
– given up to the moment
– given up to the passion
– given up to the creation
trusting my own capacity for transformation

UNTITLED

song in the silence
irrepressible laughter
long peace

let go
let go
let go
always let go

always receive

SOURCES AND ACKNOWLEDGEMENTS

Real – first published in *Struggles to Love: The Spirituality of the Beatitudes*, Kathy Galloway, SPCK, 1994, ISBN 0281047405. Used by permission of SPCK.

Heredity – first published in *A Scottish Childhood, Volume II*, compiled by Nancy E.M. Bailey for Save the Children, Harper Collins Publishers, Glasgow, 1998, ISBN 0004721764.

Edinburgh Vignette – first published in *A Scottish Childhood, Volume II*, compiled by Nancy E.M. Bailey for Save the Children, Harper Collins Publishers, Glasgow, 1998, ISBN 0004721764.

A Map of Bread – first published in *The One Loaf: An Everyday Celebration*, Joy Mead, Wild Goose Publications, 2000, ISBN 1901557383.

Drawing the Lines of Engagement – first published in *A Story to Live By*, Kathy Galloway, SPCK, 1999, ISBN 028105164X. Used by permission of SPCK. Also reprinted by permission of The Pilgrim Press, Cleveland 1999.

Open Warfare – first published in *A Story to Live By*, Kathy Galloway, SPCK, 1999, ISBN 028105164X. Used by permission of SPCK. Also reprinted by permission of The Pilgrim Press, Cleveland 1999.

De-contamination – first published in *A Story to Live By*, Kathy Galloway, SPCK, 1999, ISBN 028105164X. Used by permission of SPCK. Also reprinted by permission of The Pilgrim Press, Cleveland 1999.

Cross-border Peace Talks – first published in *Pushing the Boat Out*, Kathy Galloway (ed), Wild Goose Publications, 1995, ISBN 0947988742.

Visual design for 'Peace Processes' sequence by Kathy Galloway and David Galloway. Drawings by David Galloway.

Map used in the poem 'Drawing the Lines of Engagement' – from *Baedeker's AA: Middle East*, ISBN 3-920339-60-6. Official map of Nah-und Mittelost-Verein e.V, D-2000 Hamburg 13, Bundesrepublik Deutschland. © VWK. Ryborsch GmbH, verlag für wirtschafts – und kartographie-publikationnen. Current copyright holder unknown.

Map used in the poem 'Balancing Act' – from *World Travel Map: Israel with Jordan*, ISBN 0 7028 0239 5. © Collins Bartholomew Ltd 1990. Used by permission of Harper Collins, Glasgow, UK.

Map used in the poem 'Preliminary Sketches' – from *Afrika (Africa) Hallwag*, ISBN 3 444 00011 1 © C Hallwag Kummerly+Frey AG, CH-3322 Schonbuhl-Bern, Switzerland. Used by permission of Hallwag Kummerley+Frey.

Map used in the poem 'Open Warfare' – from *World Travel Map: Israel with Jordan*, ISBN 0 7028 0239 5. © Collins Bartholomew Ltd 1990. Used by permission of Harper Collins, Glasgow, UK.

Map used in the poem 'Counting the Dead' – from *Afrika (Africa) Hallwag*, ISBN 3 444 00011 1 © C Hallwag Kummerly+Frey AG, CH-3322 Schonbuhl-Bern, Switzerland. Used by permission of Hallwag Kummerley+Frey.

Map used in the poem 'Ceasefire' – from *Collins Atlas of the World: New Nations Edition*, first published 1983 by William Collins Sons & Co Ltd, 4th edition 1993, ISBN 0 00 448038 4 © Collins Bartholomew Ltd, 1983. Used by permission of Harper Collins, Glasgow, UK.

Map used in the poem 'The New State' – from *Afrika (Africa) Hallwag*, ISBN 3 444 00011 1 © C Hallwag Kummerly+Frey AG, CH-3322 Schonbuhl-Bern, Switzerland. Used by permission of Hallwag Kummerley+Frey.

Map used in the poem 'De-contamination' – from *Collins Atlas of the World: New Nations Edition*, first published 1983 by William Collins Sons & Co Ltd, 4th edition 1993, ISBN 0 00 448038 4 © Collins Bartholomew Ltd, 1983. Used by permission of Harper Collins, Glasgow, UK.

Map used in the poem 'Allies' – from *Peters World Map*, ISBN 1-85365-305-5 © Akademische Verlagsanstalt, Vaduz. Used by permission of Oxford Cartographers, Oxford, UK.

Map used in the poem 'Reconstruction' – from *Collins Atlas of the World: New Nations Edition*, first published 1983 by William Collins Sons & Co Ltd, 4th edition 1993, ISBN 0 00 448038 4 © Collins Bartholomew Ltd 1983. Used by permission of Harper Collins, Glasgow, UK.

The Crack – first published in *Struggles to Love: The Spirituality of the Beatitudes*, Kathy Galloway, SPCK, 1994, ISBN 0281047405. Used by permission of SPCK.

The Line, The Line too – first published in *Pushing the Boat Out*, Kathy Galloway (ed), Wild Goose Publications, 1995, ISBN 0947988742.

There Will Be Peace, Let Us Be Different, Going Over, Coming to Jerusalem sequence, Christ of Scotland – first published in *Love Burning Deep: Poems and Lyrics*, Kathy Galloway, SPCK, 1993, ISBN 0281046425. Out of print. Used by permission of SPCK.

The Story So Far – first published in *A Story to Live By*, Kathy Galloway, SPCK, 1999, ISBN 028105164X. Used by permission of SPCK . Also reprinted by permission of The Pilgrim Press, Cleveland 1999.

Camas Poems – first published in *After the Watergaw*, edited by Robert Davidson, Scottish Cultural Press, 1998, ISBN 1840170247.

Manna from Heaven – first published in *The Flow ... Poetry from Camas*, edited by Rachel McCann, 2003.

Remember Me – first published in the *ATD Fourth World Journal*. ATD Fourth World is an international Non-Governmental Organisation (NGO) that engages with individuals and institutions to acknowledge and support the daily efforts of people in extreme poverty [*from the ATD Fourth World web site*].

Rejoicing in Heaven – first published in *Struggles to Love*, Kathy Galloway, SPCK, 1994, ISBN 0281047405. Used by permission of SPCK.

In That Place – first published in *A Story to Live By*, Kathy Galloway, SPCK, 1999, ISBN 028105164X. Used by permission of SPCK. Also reprinted by permission of The Pilgrim Press, Cleveland 1999.

Dreaming of Eden (i,ii,iii) – first published in *Dreaming of Eden: Reflections on Christianity and Sexuality*, Wild Goose Publications, Kathy Galloway, ISBN 0947988513, 1997.

Human – first published in *Celebrating Women*, Hannah Ward, Jennifer Wild, Janet Morley (editors), SPCK, 1995, ISBN 0281048363.

INDEX OF TITLES

The Pattern of Our Days

Liturgies and resources for worship from the Iona Community

Kathy Galloway (ed)

This inspiring anthology reflecting the life and witness of the Iona Community is intended to encourage creativity in worship. Includes liturgies of pilgrimage, healing and acts of witness and dissent; prayers, reflections, readings, meditations, etc.

1996 • ISBN 0 947988 76 9

Dreaming of Eden

Reflections on Christianity and sexuality

Kathy Galloway (ed)

Sexuality as life journey, including:
– Christianity and sexual violence
– Impact of feminism and gay thought on male heterosexuality
– Incarnating feminist theology
– Reconstruction and deconstruction of marriage
– Celibacy: a subversive proclamation of Christian freedom, or sexual repression?

1998 • ISBN 0 947988 51 3

Praying for the Dawn

A resource book for the ministry of healing

Ruth Burgess & Kathy Galloway (eds)

A compilation of material from several writers, with strong emphasis on liturgies and resources for healing services. Includes a section on how to introduce healing services to those who may not be familiar with them.

2000 • ISBN 1 901557 26 X

Pushing the Boat Out

New poetry

Kathy Galloway (ed)

A collection of poetry by writers involved in the justice and peace spirituality of the Iona Community.

1995 • ISBN 0 947988 74 2

THE IONA COMMUNITY

The Iona Community, founded in 1938 by the Revd George MacLeod, then a parish minister in Glasgow, is an ecumenical Christian community committed to seeking new ways of living the Gospel in today's world. Initially working to restore part of the medieval abbey on Iona, the Community today remains committed to 'rebuilding the common life' through working for social and political change, striving for the renewal of the church with an ecumenical emphasis, and exploring new, more inclusive approaches to worship, all based on an integrated understanding of spirituality.

The Community now has over 240 Members, about 1500 Associate Members and around 1500 Friends. The Members – women and men from many denominations and backgrounds (lay and ordained), living throughout Britain with a few overseas – are committed to a fivefold Rule of devotional discipline, sharing and accounting for use of time and money, regular meeting, and action for justice and peace.

At the Community's three residential centres – the Abbey and the MacLeod Centre on Iona, and Camas Adventure Camp on the Ross of Mull – guests are welcomed from March to October and over Christmas. Hospitality is provided for over 110 people, along with a unique opportunity, usually through week-long programmes, to extend horizons and forge relationships through sharing an experience of the common life in worship, work, discussion and relaxation. The Community's shop on Iona, just outside the Abbey grounds, carries an attractive range of books and craft goods.

The Community's administrative headquarters are in Glasgow, which also serves as a base for its work with young people, the Wild Goose Resource Group working in the field of worship, a bi-monthly magazine, *Coracle*, and a publishing house, Wild Goose Publications.

For information on the Iona Community contact:
The Iona Community, Fourth Floor, Savoy House, 140 Sauchiehall Street,
Glasgow G2 3DH, UK. Phone: 0141 332 6343
e-mail: ionacomm@gla.iona.org.uk; web: www.iona.org.uk

For enquiries about visiting Iona, please contact:
Iona Abbey, Isle of Iona, Argyll PA76 6SN, UK. Phone: 01681 700404
e-mail: ionacomm@iona.org.uk